STUDENT WORKBOOK
VOLUME 2

PHYSICS

FOR SCIENTISTS AND ENGINEERS

A STRATEGIC APPROACH

Randall D. Knight

California Polytechnic State University
San Luis Obispo

PEARSON

Addison
Wesley

San Francisco   Boston   New York
Capetown   Hong Kong   London   Madrid   Mexico City
Montreal   Munich   Paris   Singapore   Sydney   Tokyo   Toronto

Table of Contents

Preface

Learning physics, just as learning any skill, requires regular practice of the basic techniques. That is what this *Student Workbook* is all about. The workbook consists of exercises that give you an opportunity to practice the ideas and techniques presented in the textbook and in class. These exercises are intended to be done on a daily basis, right after the topics have been discussed in class and are still fresh in your mind.

You will find that the exercises are nearly all *qualitative* rather than *quantitative*. They ask you to draw pictures, interpret graphs, use ratios, write short explanations, or provide other answers that do not involve significant calculations. The purpose of these exercises is to help you develop the basic thinking tools you'll later need for quantitative problem solving. Successful completion of the workbook exercises will prepare you to tackle the more quantitative end-of-chapter homework problems in the textbook. It is highly recommended that you do the workbook exercises *before* starting the end-of-chapter problems.

You will find that the exercises in this workbook are keyed to specific sections of the textbook in order to let you practice the new ideas introduced in that section. You should keep the text beside you as you work and refer to it often. You will usually find Tactics Boxes, figures, or examples in the textbook that are directly relevant to the exercises. When asked to draw figures or diagrams, you should attempt to draw them so that they look much like the figures and diagrams in the textbook.

Because the exercises go with specific sections of the text, you should answer them on the basis of information presented in *just* that section (and prior sections). You may have learned new ideas in Section 7 of a chapter, but you should not use those ideas when answering questions from Section 4. There will be ample opportunity in the Section 7 exercises to use that information there.

You will need a few "tools" to complete the exercises. Many of the exercises will ask you to *color code* your answers by drawing some items in black, others in red, and yet others in blue. You need to purchase a few colored pencils to do this. The author highly recommends that you work in pencil, rather than ink, so that you can easily erase. Few people produce work so free from errors that they can work in ink! In addition, you'll find that a small, easily-carried six-inch ruler will come in handy for drawings and graphs.

As you work your way through the textbook and this workbook, you will find that physics is a way of *thinking* about how the world works and why things happen as they do. We will be interested primarily in finding relationships and seeking explanations, only secondarily in computing numerical answers. In many ways, the thinking tools developed in this workbook are what the course is all about. If you take the time to do these exercises regularly and to review the answers, in whatever form your instructor provides them, you will be well on your way to success in physics.

To the instructor: The exercises in this workbook can be used in many ways. You can have students work on some exercises in class as part of an active-learning strategy. Or you can do the same in recitation sections or laboratories. This approach allows you to discuss the answers immediately, to answer student questions, and to improvise follow-up exercises when needed. Having the students work in small groups (2 to 4 students) is highly recommended.

Alternatively, the exercises can be assigned as homework. The pages are perforated for easy tear-out, and the page breaks are in logical places so that you can assign the sections of a chapter that you would likely cover in one day of class. Exercises should be assigned immediately after presenting the relevant information in class and should be due at the beginning of the next class. Collecting them at the beginning of class, then going over two or three that are likely to cause difficulty, is an effective means of quickly reviewing major concepts from the previous class and launching a new discussion.

If the exercises are used as homework, it is *essential* for students to receive *prompt* feedback. Ideally this would occur by having the exercises graded, with written comments, and returned at the next class meeting. Posting the answers on a course website also works. Lack of prompt feedback can negate much of the value of these exercises. Placing similar qualitative/ graphical questions on quizzes and exams, and telling students at the beginning of the term that you will do so, encourages students to take the exercises seriously and to check the answers.

The author has been successful with assigning *all* exercises in the workbook as homework, collecting and grading them every day through Chapter 4, then collecting and grading them on about one-third of subsequent days on a random basis. Student feedback from end-of-term questionnaires reveals three prevalent attitudes toward the workbook exercises:

i. They think it is an unreasonable amount of work.

ii. They agree that the assignments force them to keep up and not get behind.

iii. They recognize, by the end of the term, that the workbook is a valuable learning tool.

However you choose to use these exercises, they will significantly strengthen your students' conceptual understanding of physics.

Answers to all workbook exercises are provided as pdf files on the *Instructor's Supplement* CD-ROM. The author gratefully acknowledges the careful work of answer writers Professor James H. Andrew of Youngstown State University (Chapters 1–15 and 20–24) and Professor Susan Cable of Central Florida Community College (Chapters 16–19 and 25–42).

Acknowledgments: Many thanks to Craig Johnson, Simmy Cover, and Jean Lake for handling the production of the *Student Workbook*.

16 A Macroscopic Description of Matter

16.1 Solids, Liquids, and Gases

1. A 1×10^{-3} m^3 chunk of material has a mass of 3 kg.

   a. What is the material's density?

   b. Would a 2×10^{-3} m^3 chunk of the same material have the same mass? Explain.

   c. Would a 2×10^{-3} m^3 chunk of the same material have the same density? Explain.

2. You are given an irregularly-shaped chunk of material and asked to find its density. List the *specific* steps that you would follow to do so.

3. Object 1 has an irregular shape. Its density is 4000 kg/m^3.

   a. Object 2 has the same shape and dimensions as object 1, but it is twice as massive. What is the density of object 2?

   b. Object 3 has the same mass and the same *shape* as object 1, but its size in all three dimensions is twice that of object 1. What is the density of object 3?

16.2 Atoms and Moles

4. You have 100 g of aluminum and 100 g of lead.
   a. Which has the greater volume? Explain.

   b. Which contains a larger number of moles? Explain.

   c. Which contains more atoms? Explain.

5. A cylinder contains 2 g of oxygen gas. A piston is used to compress the gas. After the gas has been compressed:
   a. Has the mass of the gas increased, decreased, or not changed? Explain.

   b. Has the density of the gas increased, decreased, or not changed? Explain.

   c. Have the number of moles of gas increased, decreased, or not changed? Explain.

   d. Has the number density of the gas increased, decreased, or not changed? Explain.

16.3 Temperature

6. Rank in order, from highest to lowest, the temperatures $T_1 = 0$ K, $T_2 = 0°C$, and $T_3 = 0°F$.

7. "Room temperature" is often considered to be 68°F. What is room temperature in °C and in K?

8. a. The gas pressure inside a sealed, rigid container is 1 atm at 100K. What is the pressure at 200K?

   b. The gas pressure inside a sealed, rigid container is 1 atm at 100°C. What is the pressure at 200°C?

16.4 Phase Changes

9. On the phase diagram:

   a. Draw *and label* a line to show a process in which the substance boils at constant pressure. Be sure to include an arrowhead on your line to show the direction of the process.

   b. Draw *and label* a line to show a process in which the substance freezes at constant temperature.

   c. Draw *and label* a line to show a process in which the substance sublimates at constant pressure.

   d. Draw a small circle around the critical point.

   e. Draw a small box around the triple point.

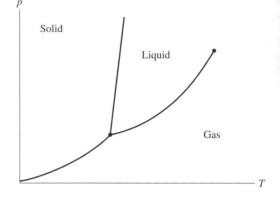

10. The figure shows the phase diagram of water. Answer the following questions by referring to the phase diagram and, perhaps, drawing lines on the phase diagram.

    a. What happens to the boiling-point temperature of water as you go to higher and higher elevations in the mountains?

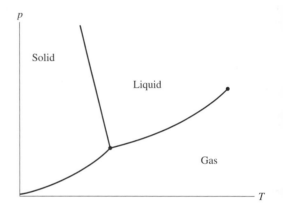

    b. Suppose you place a beaker of liquid water at 20°C in a vacuum chamber and then steadily reduce the pressure. What, if anything, happens to the water?

    c. Is ice less dense or more dense than liquid water?

16.5 Ideal Gases

11. It is well known that you can trap liquid in a drinking straw by placing the tip of your finger over the top while the straw is in the liquid, then lifting it out. The liquid runs out when you release your finger.

    a. What is the *net* force on the cylinder of trapped liquid?

    b. Draw a free-body diagram for the trapped liquid. Label each vector.

    c. Is the gas pressure inside the straw, between the liquid and your finger, greater than, less than, or equal to atmospheric pressure? Explain.

    d. If your answer to part c was "greater" or "less," how did the pressure change from the atmospheric pressure that was present when you placed your finger over the top of the straw?

12. A gas is in a sealed container. By what factor does the gas pressure change if:
    a. The volume is doubled and the temperature is tripled?

    b. The volume is halved and the temperature is tripled?

13. A gas is in a sealed container. By what factor does the gas temperature change if:
    a. The volume is doubled and the pressure is tripled?

    b. The volume is halved and the pressure is tripled?

14. The gas inside in a cylinder is heated, causing a piston in the cylinder to move outward. The heating causes the temperature to double and the length of the cylinder to triple. By what factor does the gas pressure change?

15. A gas is in a sealed container. The gas pressure is tripled and the temperature is doubled.
    a. What happens to the number of moles of gas in the container?

    b. What happens to the number density of the gas in the container?

16.6 Ideal Gas Processes

16. The graphs below show the initial state of a gas. Draw a *pV* diagram showing the following processes:

   a. An isochoric process that doubles the pressure.

   b. An isobaric process that doubles the temperature.

   c. An isothermal process that halves the volume.

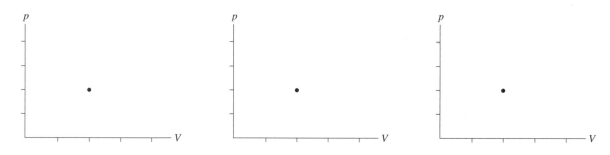

17. Interpret the *pV* diagrams shown below by
   a. Naming the process.
   b. Stating the *factors* by which *p*, *V*, and *T* change. (A fixed quantity changes by a factor of 1.)

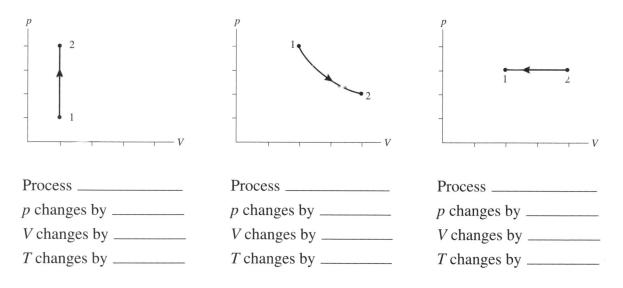

Process _____

p changes by _____

V changes by _____

T changes by _____

Process _____

p changes by _____

V changes by _____

T changes by _____

Process _____

p changes by _____

V changes by _____

T changes by _____

18. Starting from the initial state shown, draw a *pV* diagram for the three-step process:

   i.   An isochoric process that halves the temperature,

   ii. An isothermal process that halves the pressure, then

   iii. An isobaric process that doubles the volume.

   Label each of the stages on your diagram.

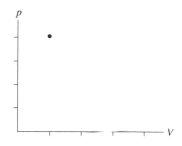

17 Work, Heat, and the First Law of Thermodynamics

17.1 It's All About Energy

17.2 Work in Ideal-Gas Processes

1. How much work is done on the gas in each of the following processes?

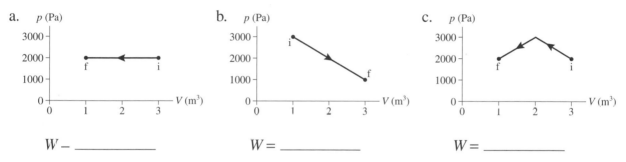

a.

b.

c.

$W -$ _____ $W =$ _____ $W =$ _____

2. The figure below shows a process in which a gas is compressed from 300 cm³ to 100 cm³.

   a. Use the middle set of axes to draw the *pV* diagram of a process that starts from initial state i, compresses the gas to 100 cm³, and does the same amount of work on the gas as the process on the left.

   b. Is there an isochoric process that does the same amount of work on the gas as the process on the left? If so, show it on the axes on the right. If not, use the blank space of the axes to explain why.

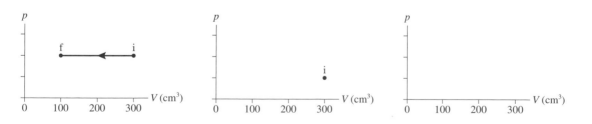

3. The figure shows a process in which work is done to compress a gas.

   a. Draw and label a process A that starts and ends at the same points but does *more* work on the gas

   b. Draw and label a process B that starts and ends at the same points but does *less* work on the gas.

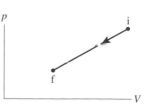

17.3 Heat

17.4 The First Law of Thermodynamics

4. When the space shuttle returns to earth, its surfaces get very hot as it passes through the atmosphere at high speed.

    a. Has the space shuttle been heated? If so, what was the source of the heat? If not, why is it hot?

    b. Energy must be conserved. What happens to the space shuttle's initial kinetic energy?

5. Cold water is poured into a hot metal container.

    a. What physical quantities can you *measure* that tell you that the metal and water are somehow changing?

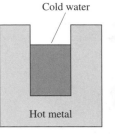
Cold water

Hot metal

    b. What is the condition for equilibrium, after which no additional changes take place?

    c. Use the concept of energy to describe how the metal and the water interact.

    d. Is your description in part c something that you can *observe* happening? Or is it an *inference* based on the measurements you specified in part a?

6. Do each of the following describe a property of a system, an interaction of a system with its environment, or both? Explain.

   a. Temperature:

   b. Heat:

   c. Thermal energy:

7. a. For each of the following processes:

   i.   Is the value of the work W, the heat Q, and the change of thermal energy ΔE_{th} positive (+), negative (−) or zero (0)?

   ii. Does the temperature increase (+), decrease (−), or not change (0)?

	W	Q	ΔE_{th}	ΔT
You hit a nail with a hammer.	____	____	____	____
You hold a nail over a Bunsen burner.	____	____	____	____
You compress the air in a bicycle pump by pushing down on the handle very rapidly.	____	____	____	____
You turn on a flame under a cylinder of gas, and the gas undergoes an isothermal expansion.	____	____	____	____
A flame turns liquid water into steam.	____	____	____	____
High-pressure steam spins a turbine.	____	____	____	____
Steam contacts a cold surface and condenses.	____	____	____	____
A moving crate slides to a halt on a rough surface.	____	____	____	____
High-pressure gas in a cylinder pushes a piston outward very rapidly.	____	____	____	____

   b. Are each of your responses consistent with the first law of thermodynamics? If not, which ones are not?

8. The text says that the first law of thermodynamics is simply a general statement of the idea of conservation of energy. What does this mean? How does the first law embody the idea of energy conservation?

9. Consider an ideal-gas process that increases the volume of the gas in a cylinder without changing its pressure.

   a. Show the process on a pV diagram.

   b. Show the process on a first-law bar chart.

   c. What kind of process is this? _____

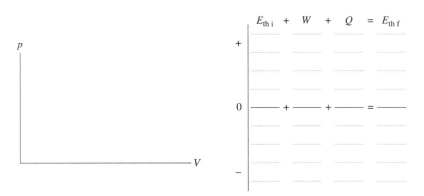

10. Consider an ideal-gas process that increases the pressure of the gas in a cylinder without changing its temperature.

   a. Show the process on a pV diagram.

   b. Show the process on a first-law bar chart.

   c. What kind of process is this? _____

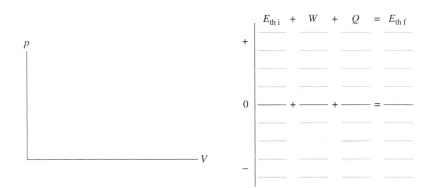

17.5 Thermal Properties of Matter

17.6 Calorimetry

11. A beaker of water at 80.0°C is placed in the center of a large, well-insulated room whose air temperature is 20.0°C. Is the final temperature of the water:

   i.   20.0°C.
   ii. Slightly above 20.0°C.
   iii. 50.0°C.

   iv. Slightly less than 80.0°C.
   v.   80.0°C.

   Explain.

12. Materials A and B have equal densities, but A has a larger specific heat than B. You have 100 g cubes of each material.

   a. Cube A, initially at 0°C, is placed in good thermal contact with cube B, initially at 200°C. The cubes are inside a well-insulated container where they don't interact with their surroundings. Is their final temperature greater than, less than, or equal to 100°C? Explain.

   b. Cube A and cube B are both heated to 200°C, then placed on a table in room-temperature air. Which one cools down more quickly? Explain.

13. 100 g of ice at 0°C and 100 g of steam at 100°C interact thermally in a well-insulated container. Is the final state of the system

   i.   An ice-water mixture at 0°C?
   ii. Water at a temperature between 0°C and 50°C?
   iii. Water at 50°C?
   iv. Water at a temperature between 50°C and 100°C?
   v.   A water-steam mixture at 100°C?

   Explain.

17.7 The Specific Heats of Gases

14. Two containers hold equal masses of nitrogen gas at equal temperatures. You supply 10 J of heat to container A while not allowing its volume to change, and you supply 10 J of heat to container B while not allowing its pressure to change. Afterward, is temperature T_A greater than, less than, or equal to T_B? Explain.

15. You need to raise the temperature of a gas by 10°C. To use the least amount of heat energy, should you heat the gas at constant pressure or at constant volume? Explain.

16. Describe *why* the molar specific heat at constant pressure is larger than the molar specific heat at constant volume.

17. The figure shows an adiabatic process.

    a. Is the final temperature higher than, lower than, or equal to the initial temperature?

    b. Draw *and label* the T_i and T_f isotherms on the figure.

    c. Is the work done on the gas positive or negative? Explain.

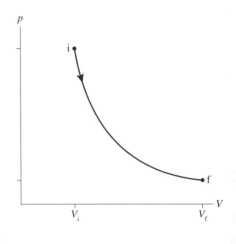

    d. Show *on the figure* how you would determine the amount of work done.

    e. Is any heat energy added to or removed from the system in this process? Explain.

    f. *Why* does the gas temperature change?

18 The Micro/Macro Connection

18.1 Molecular Collisions

1. a. Solids and liquids resist being compressed. They are not totally incompressible, but it takes large forces to compress them even slightly. If it is true that matter consists of atoms, what can you infer about the microscopic nature of solids and liquids from their incompressibility?

   b. Solids, and to a lesser extent liquids, also resist being pulled apart. You can break a metal or glass rod by pulling the ends in opposite directions, but it takes a large force to do so. What can you infer from this observation about the properties of atoms?

2. a. Gases, in contrast with solids and liquids, are very compressible. What can you infer from this observation about the microscopic nature of gases?

   b. The density of air at STP is about $\frac{1}{1000}$ the density of water. How does the average distance between air molecules compare to the average distance between water molecules? Explain.

3. a. Can you think of any everyday experiences or observations that would suggest that the molecules of a gas are in constant, *random* motion? (Note: The existence of "wind" is *not* such an observation. Wind implies that the gas as a whole can move, but it doesn't tell you anything about the motions of the individual molecules in the gas.)

  b. If the molecules are moving randomly and colliding with each other, do you expect there to be a very wide range of molecular speeds? Or do you expect that most of the molecules will have very similar speeds? Explain.

4. The mean free path of molecules in a gas is 200 nm.
  a. What will be the mean free path if the pressure is doubled while all other state variables are held constant?

  b. What will be the mean free path if the absolute temperature is doubled while all other state variables are held constant?

5. Helium has atomic mass number $A = 4$. Neon has $A = 20$ and argon has $A = 40$. Rank in order, from largest to smallest, the mean free paths λ_{He}, λ_{Ne}, and λ_{Ar} at STP. Explain.

18.2 Pressure in a Gas

6. If the pressure of a gas is really due to the *random* collisions of molecules with the walls of the container, why do pressure gauges—even very sensitive ones—give perfectly steady readings? Shouldn't the gauge be continually jiggling and fluctuating? Explain.

7. According to kinetic theory, the pressure of a gas depends on the number density and the rms speed of the gas molecules. Consider a sealed container of gas that is heated at constant volume.

   a. According to the ideal gas law, does the pressure of the gas increase or stay the same? Explain.

   b. Does the number density of the gas increase or stay the same? Explain.

   c. What can you infer from these observations about a relationship between the gas temperature (a macroscopic parameter) and the rms speed of the molecules (a microscopic parameter)?

8. Suppose you could suddenly increase the speed of every molecule in a gas by a factor of 2.
   a. Would the rms speed of the molecules increase by a factor of $(2)^{1/2}$, 2, or 2^2? Explain.

   b. Would the gas pressure increase by a factor of $(2)^{1/2}$, 2, or 2^2? Explain.

18.3 Temperature

9. If you double the temperature of a gas:

   a. Does the average translational kinetic energy per molecule change? If so, by what factor?

   b. Does the root-mean-square velocity of the molecules change? If so, by what factor?

10. Lithium vapor, which is produced by heating lithium to the relatively low boiling point of 1340°C, forms a gas of Li_2 molecules. Each molecule has a molecular mass of 14 u. The molecules in nitrogen gas (N_2) have a molecular mass of 28 u. If the Li_2 and N_2 gases are at the same temperature, which of the following is true?

    i. v_{rms} of $N_2 = 2.00 \times v_{rms}$ of Li_2.
    ii. v_{rms} of $N_2 = 1.41 \times v_{rms}$ of Li_2.
    iii. v_{rms} of $N_2 = v_{rms}$ of Li_2.
    iv. v_{rms} of $N_2 = 0.71 \times v_{rms}$ of Li_2.
    v. v_{rms} of $N_2 = 0.50 \times v_{rms}$ of Li_2.

    Explain.

11. Suppose you could suddenly increase the speed of every molecule in a gas by a factor of 2. Would the temperature of the gas increase by a factor of $(2)^{1/2}$, 2, or 2^2? Explain.

12. Two gases have the same number density and the same distribution of speeds. The molecules of gas 2 are more massive than the molecules of gas 1.

    a. Do the two gases have the same pressure? If not, which is larger?

    b. Do the two gases have the same temperature? If not, which is larger?

13. a. What is the average translational kinetic energy of a gas at absolute zero?

    b. Can a molecule have negative translational kinetic energy? Explain.

    c. Based on your answers to parts a and b, what is the translational kinetic energy of *every* molecule in the gas?

    d. Would it be physically possible for the thermal energy of a gas to be less than its thermal energy at absolute zero? Explain.

    e. Is it possible to have a temperature less than absolute zero? Explain.

18.4 Thermal Energy and Specific Heat

18.5 Thermal Interactions and Heat

14. Suppose you could suddenly increase the speed of every molecule in a gas by a factor of 2.
    a. Does the thermal energy of the gas change? If so, by what factor? If not, why not?

    b. Does the molar specific heat change? If so, by what factor? If not, why not?

15. Hot water is poured into a cold container. Give a *microscopic* description of how these two systems interact until they reach thermal equilibrium.

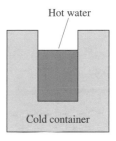

16. A beaker of cold water is placed over a flame.
    a. What *is* a flame?

    b. Give a *microscopic* description of how the flame increases the water temperature.

17. The *rapid* compression of a gas by a fast-moving piston increases the gas temperature. For example, you likely have noticed that pumping up a bicycle tire causes the bottom of the pump to get warm. Consider a gas that is rapidly compressed by a piston.

a. Does the thermal energy of the gas increase or stay the same? Explain.

b. Is there a transfer of heat energy to the gas? Explain.

c. Is work done on the gas? Explain.

d. Give a *microscopic* description of why the gas temperature increases as the piston moves in.

18. A container with 0.1 mol of helium ($A = 4$) and a container with 0.2 mol of argon ($A = 40$) are placed in thermal contact with each other. The helium has an initial temperature of 200°C and the argon has an initial temperature of 0°C. *After* they have reached thermal equilibrium:

0.1 mol He	0.2 mol Ar
200°C	0°C

a. Is v_{rms} of helium greater than, less than, or equal to v_{rms} of argon? Explain.

b. Does the helium have more thermal energy than, less thermal energy than, or the same amount of thermal energy as the argon? Explain.

18.6 Irreversible Processes and the Second Law of Thermodynamics

19. Every cubic meter of air contains ≈250,000 J of thermal energy. This is approximately the kinetic energy of a car going 50 mph. Even though it might be difficult to do, could a clever engineer design a car that uses the thermal energy already in the air as "fuel"? Even if only 1% of the thermal energy could be "extracted" from the air, it would take only ≈100 m^3 of air—the volume of a typical living room in a house—to get the car up to speed. Is this idea possible? Or does it violate the laws of physics?

20. If you place a jar of perfume in the center of a room and remove the stopper, you will soon be able to smell the perfume throughout the room. If you wait long enough, will all the perfume molecules ever be back in the jar at the same time? Why or why not?

21. Suppose you place an ice cube in a cup of room-temperature water and then seal them in a well-insulated container. No energy can enter or leave the container.

    a. If you open the container an hour later, which do you expect to find: a cup of water, slightly cooler than room temperature, or a large ice cube and some 100°C steam?

    b. Finding a large ice cube and some 100°C steam would not violate the first law of thermodynamics. $W = 0$ J and $Q = 0$ J, because the container is sealed, and $\Delta E_{th} = 0$ J because the increase in thermal energy of the water molecules that have become steam is offset by the decrease in water molecules that have turned to ice. Energy is conserved, yet we never see a process like this. Why not?

19 Heat Engines and Refrigerators

19.1 Turning Heat into Work

19.2 Heat Engines and Refrigerators

1. The figure on the left shows a thermodynamic process in which a gas expands from 100 cm^3 to 300 cm^3. On the right, draw the pV diagram of a process that starts from state i, expands to 300 cm^3, and does the same amount of work as the process on the left.

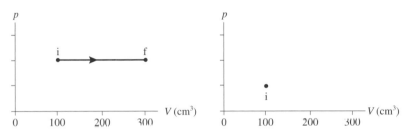

2. For each of these processes, is work done *by* the system ($W < 0$, $W_s > 0$), *on* the system ($W > 0$, $W_s < 0$), or is *no* work done?

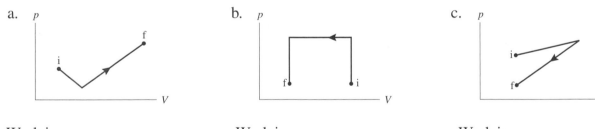

a. Work is _____

b. Work is _____

c. Work is _____

3. Rank in order, from largest to smallest, the thermal efficiencies η_1 to η_4 of these heat engines.

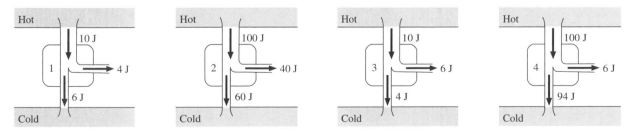

Order:

Explanation:

4. Could you have a heat engine with $\eta > 1$? Explain.

5. For each engine shown,
    a. Supply the missing value.
    b. Determine the thermal efficiency.

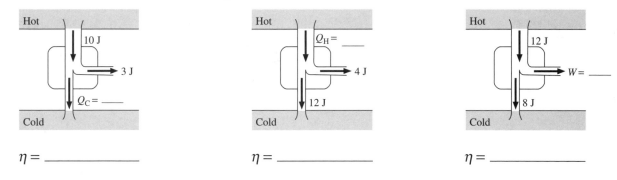

$\eta = $ _____ $\eta = $ _____ $\eta = $ _____

6. For each refrigerator shown,
    a. Supply the missing value.
    b. Determine the coefficient of performance.

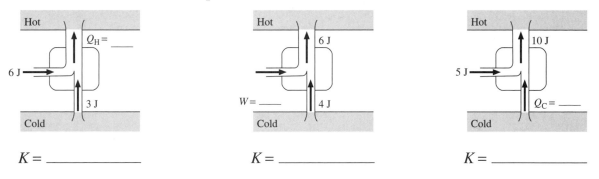

$K = $ _____ $K = $ _____ $K = $ _____

7. Does a refrigerator do work in order to cool the interior? Explain.

19.3 Ideal-Gas Heat Engines

8. Starting from the point shown, draw a pV diagram for the following processes.

a. An isobaric process in which work is done *by* the system.

b. An adiabatic process in which work is done *on* the system.

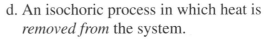

c. An isothermal process in which heat is *added to* the system.

d. An isochoric process in which heat is *removed from* the system.

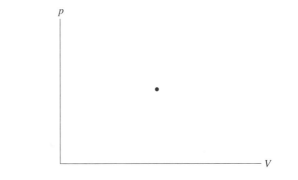

9. Rank in order, from largest to smallest, the amount of work W_1 to W_4 done by the gas in each of these cycles.

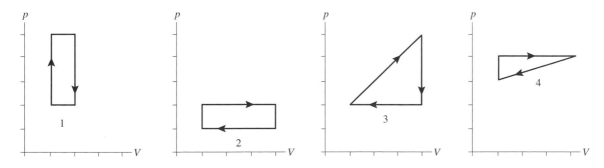

Order:

Explanation:

10. The figure uses a series of pictures to illustrate a thermodynamic cycle.

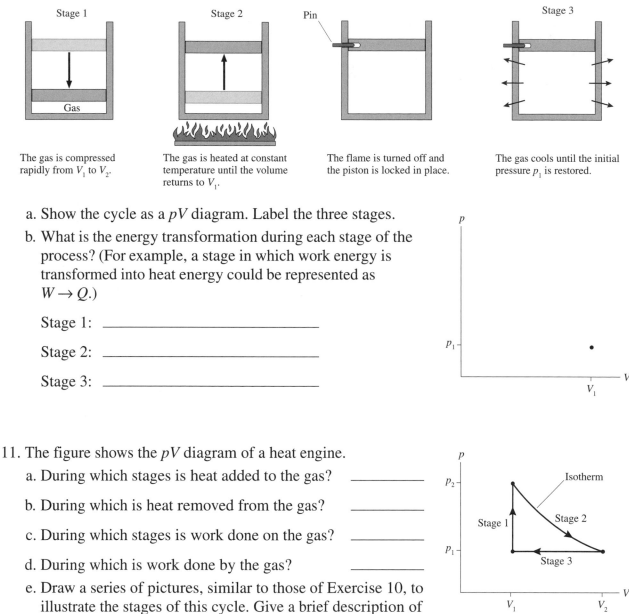

a. Show the cycle as a pV diagram. Label the three stages.

b. What is the energy transformation during each stage of the process? (For example, a stage in which work energy is transformed into heat energy could be represented as $W \rightarrow Q$.)

Stage 1: _____

Stage 2: _____

Stage 3: _____

11. The figure shows the pV diagram of a heat engine.

a. During which stages is heat added to the gas? _____

b. During which is heat removed from the gas? _____

c. During which stages is work done on the gas? _____

d. During which is work done by the gas? _____

e. Draw a series of pictures, similar to those of Exercise 10, to illustrate the stages of this cycle. Give a brief description of what happens during each stage.

12. A heat engine satisfies $W_{out} = Q_{net}$. Why is there no ΔE_{th} term in this relationship?

13. Two thermodynamic cycles are shown. Which cycle has a larger thermal efficiency? Explain.

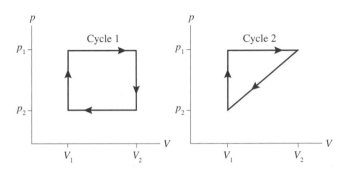

14. Two thermodynamic cycles are shown. Which cycle has a larger thermal efficiency? Explain.

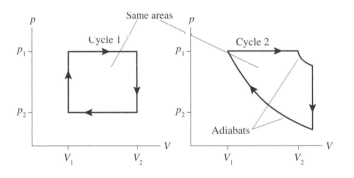

19.4 Ideal-Gas Refrigerators

15. a. The figure shows the pV diagram of a heat engine.

    During which stages is heat added to the gas? _____

    During which is heat removed from the gas? _____

    During which stages is work done on the gas? _____

    During which is work done by the gas? _____

    Circle the answers that complete the sentence:
    The temperature of the hot reservoir must be

    i. >   ii. =   iii. <

    the temperature i. T_2 ii. T_3 iii. T_4

    Circle the answers that complete the sentence: The temperature of the cold reservoir must be

    i. >   ii. =   iii. <

    the temperature i. T_2 ii. T_1 iii. T_4

    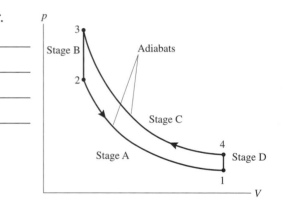

    b. The figure shows the pV diagram of a refrigerator.

    During which stages is heat added to the gas? _____

    During which is heat removed from the gas? _____

    During which stages is work done on the gas? _____

    During which is work done by the gas? _____

    Circle the answers that complete the sentence:
    The temperature of the hot reservoir must be

    i. >   ii. =   iii. <

    the temperature i. T_2 ii. T_3 iii. T_4

    Circle the answers that complete the sentence:
    The temperature of the cold reservoir must be

    i. >   ii. =   iii. <

    the temperature i. T_2 ii. T_1 iii. T_4

16. An ideal-gas device operates with the cycle shown. Is it a refrigerator? That is, does it remove heat energy from a cold side and exhaust heat energy to a hot side? Explain.

    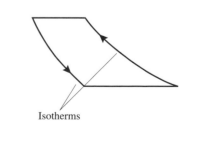

19.5 The Limits of Efficiency

19.6 The Carnot Cycle

17. Do each of the following represent a possible heat engine or refrigerator? If not, what is wrong?

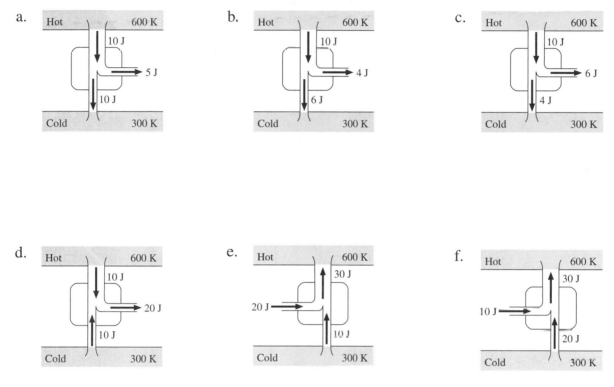

18. Four Carnot engines operate with the hot and cold reservoir temperatures shown in the table.

Engine	T_C (K)	T_H (K)
1	300	600
2	200	400
3	200	600
4	300	400

Rank in order, from largest to smallest, the thermal efficiencies η_1 to η_4 of these engines.

Order:

Explanation:

19. It gets pretty hot in your unairconditioned apartment. In browsing the internet, you find a company selling small "room air conditioners." You place it on the floor, plug it in, and—the advertisement says—the air conditioner will lower the room temperature up to 10°F. Should you order one? Explain.

Notes

Notes

Notes

Notes

Notes

Notes

Notes

Notes

Notes

Notes